EXOTIC NEUROTIC

By:

Kenneth Jarrett Singleton

ISBN: 150095196X
ISBN 13:9781500951962

CONTENTS

PUTRID BIRTH

The daffodils of youth are still smelling putrid.
They have grown beside my plastic, crucified cupid.
I wonder if they want to rot with me in my nest?
An unceasing pain in my pressured chest.

He was underdeveloped for his age.
His parents restrained him within their personal cage.
He was ungratefully nourished by way of container.
His umbilical cord spewed just like a complainer.

He was never washed spotless, or with good measure.
He never acquired, but he still sought pleasure.
'Eliminate me, please,' was his final thought.
I have long been prepared for the eternal rot.

There are constant clicks because the tube is feeding.
I hear constant clicks because his organs are bleeding.
Interminably will remain your absence of worth.
I'm providing putrid daffodils for your putrid birth.

FRUSTRATION AND VEXATION

I feel the frustration.
Experience my frustration.
I've gotten to this place on my own.
You must feel worthless.
You are entirely worthless.
I would like to use you on my own.
I am an established sinner.
I've comfirmed that I'm the winner.
I'm sitting here on my throne.

You eventually become used to being sick.
I have grown accustomed to sensing a tick.
You become used to being oppressed.
I have grown accustomed to feeling depressed.

The sensation is empty.
I am feeling so empty.
It's going to be a gloomy day.
It's obvious you are vacant.
I am glad that you are vacant.
You're as unfilled as a boring day.
It's my hope you'll always hate me.
I beg of you, despise me;
Because that means you will keep away.

You never become used to experiencing life.
I have grown accustomed to inner strife.
You never grow accustomed to sensing you're ill.
I have become used to the agency mill.

SELF-INDULGENCE

Haven't we met once before?
I think I remember when.
You used to provide an awkward disservice.
I despised you even then.
So much for the time you had.
I'm pleased that you're looking thin.

Employ the basics without trust.
Employ the basics;
If you must.
Let your friends turn into dust.
The complexity of sexual spores.
I don't want to do any of my chores.

I am lacking self-discipline.
Too much is never enough.
I'm glad that I lack self-discipline.
Did you enjoy my rebuff?
Sometimes it's hard to exist.
I guess that life's too tough.

Involve the silent without trust.
Involve the silent;
If you must.
Let your heart gradually rust.
The complexity of emotional sores.
I refuse to do any of my chores.

ATTENUATION

I'm going to display my many maladies.
You should expect multiple fatalities.
I am exultant due to what I've done.
Let's watch the corpses bake in the sun.

On display are my many realities.
You should expect numerous maladies.
Hit me in my stomach so I can shit.
Let me nurse you with my torture kit.

Lose your will.
I can't stay still.
Attenuate;
You certified ingrate.

My sex organs remain ready for reproduction.
I am tired of being in a state of obstruction.
You aren't entitled to a special delivery.
His appearance is considerably livery.

There are knots in my stomach due to the extreme tension.
When I was in school, I didn't pay attention.
The final result is always the same.
Incessant moodiness, and the spreading of blame.

Write your will.
Allow it to spill.
After the prowl;
I'll disembowel.

A GRANDIOSE REALM

A grandiose realm.
I will set fire to everyone I choose.
I cannot lose.

She will not stay.
The creeping thorns are lush today.
Slice them up anyway.
You better listen to what I have to say.

An elastic tree.
It is becoming more pliant every day.
I'm blown away.

She'll never stay.
It is simple to portray.
A mental state of disarray.
Special candies for play.

A flamboyant domain.
The estate is ostentatious.
The child was vexatious.

I would pay her to stay;
But she would refuse anyway.
Regarding me; I wish her interest would accrue.
What should I do?

A grandiose realm.
I will ignite everyone that I hate.
It's an excellent trait.

BONNIE'S DESTRUCTION OF THE PRISTINE DISHES

Long live rage, as well as, tragedy.
They'll live evermore.
I am confident without your trust.
I'm glad that life is a major whore.
She has washed her spotless dishes;
But they will never dry.
She has washed her pristine wishes;
But the promises were all lies.

Long live straining and intact notions.
Some people live life only for chores.
I am confident that you will rust.
It is now time to produce the spores.
She has left the rumor vacant.
Gossip is left for thought.
She has left the tumor vacant.
She is exactly what you are not.

I created my own discontent.
Contentment is absent and far away.
Indulging in misery without consent;
I wonder what Bonnie would say?
She possesses her own opinions.
Bonnie's judgment is viewed as fair.
She should put on display her dominion.
Long live misery and despair.

MULTIPLE ABORTIONS

I have been working.
I am constantly working.
I remember telling you to be this way.

I have been dying.
I am in the phase of dying.
I am deserving of excessive pay.

High risk, primary contortions.
Sexual feedings and multiple abortions.
I bet that you will die on your birthday.
Your daddy wants it that way.

You have been working.
You're always working.
I am glad that you overall labor well.

You find it to be useful.
You are making it useful.
Serve me before you are stale.

Altered forms with altered positions.
Suffering from multiple conditions.
A bipolar, long-distance malfunction.
Don't help me; I cannot function.

RECREATIONAL SURGEON

I am a recreational surgeon.
I would enjoy cutting your flesh.
I use various instruments.
They are medically proper.

Amalgamating, newly clogged arteries.
I'm going to remove your arteries.
Don't worry about the lung that's missing.
The diabolical hose is hissing.

I am a professional surgeon.
I am going to cut on myself.
I use numerous instruments.
They suit medical standards.

The removal of your intact body parts.
You deserve to lose your body parts.
You cry because I'm unfeeling.
It isn't my fault that I find living unappealing.

THE LUNAR PILL

The lunar pill is such a thrill.
Let's bash walls.
Enemies and centipedes;
What else crawls?
Innocence makes no sense;
In my cause.
Sugared pains' a remedy.
There's no pause.

Puppet shy;
You live a lie.
Observe the vermin;
As they shrivel and die.

The lunar pill has quite a taste.
Let's pace halls.
Alter it into a paste.
I climb walls.
Would you like to skip a step?
You weren't taught.
Nemeses for nemeses.
You've been bought.

Puppet shy.
I want you to die.
Watch your loved ones;
As they boil and cry.

INFORMAL REJECTION

Thank you so much for what you have done.
You've made me feel so well.
Thank you so much for what I have lost.
It is my hope that you burn in hell.

An everlasting state of dejection.
An everlasting form of rejection.

Allow me to express my gratitude.
My sarcastic mannerism is clear.
I have a negative attitude.
Your demeanor is completely queer.

Yet another informal rejection.
Anger due to a lack of affection.

Stare into my foggy looking glass;
You'll shatter it for sure.
Your life is ill-fated;
Because you're genetically impure.

There's another direct rejection.
Have you heard my latest objection?

Thank you so much for what you have done.
You've filled me with delight.
Thanks a lot for what I haven't won;
Another forlorn night.

INACCESSIBLE FLUIDS

As a child, I had severe headaches.
I suffered from headaches every day.
I gave birth to my dependence;
I guess it's fair to say.

The teachers gave us bad advice;
Nor did they teach any subjects well.
You've always been deaf and suffice;
I want you to bruise and swell.

Were you surprised when it was not provided?
Were you surprised at all?
Fervent self-abuse and being misguided;
My unnatural, abdominal wall.

Your fluids are inaccessible.
They're unattainable for sure.
My spasms are irrepressible.
They're impossible to insure.

CURRENT TRENDS

You are such a taxing chore.
You are making me bitter and sore.
Modern times with vivid vision.
Modern trends are my decision.

If I don't want you around;
I'll gladly put you underground.
Modern habits with modern vice.
I am happy that I'm not nice.

I'll lure you in with my bait.
Don't be scared; I'm just irate.
Current trends with a known result.
Current trends are never with fault.

You are such a taxing whore.
Your structure's rotten to it's core.
Will someone please hand me a rope?
I'm going to hang all of the people with hope.

SYNDROME E: (OR SYNDROME EXCESS)

I think I may have Syndrome E.
Syndrome E is a part of me.
I like my style.
I like my taste.
I don't let medication go to waste.

I know that I have Syndrome E.
Syndrome E is where I want to be.
Prominent styles;
They're my decision.
I stay broke with constant precision.

I'm pleased that I have Syndrome E.
Syndrome E is where you want to be.
Dominant styles;
They're my decision.
Don't attempt to alter my vision.

DESPISE LIFE

Please hate me for the rest of your days.
Express your disdain for me in various ways.
Your brain has totally been subdued.
I was one that they chose to exclude.

I am in dire need of a nemesis.
It is now time to abort.
Like you, I require a nemesis.
Emotions tend to thwart.

Despise life for the rest of your days.
Despise life in multiple ways.
I'll destroy the essentials because I can.
I'll destroy the basics to eliminate man.

I am seeking more nemeses;
Let me make my bad intentions clear.
Rid yourself of all of your appointees;
Afterwards, provide them with a sneer.

PESTILENTIAL CELL

New bodies for different measures;
You are incomplete.
New bodies for desperate measures;
You are to repeat.
I am within a pestilential cell;
Will you now alter?

You know it so well;
The tumor's constant swell.
New times;
A new treat.
Vomit well before you eat.

You'll cry teardrops of anguish;
You're getting thinner as you falter.
Despite the final result;
I refuse to fault her.
I'm occupying a pestilential cell.
I'm the last individual that you will inter.

Develop a cyst;
You will soon cease to exist.
Old times;
An old treat.
Swallow your spoiled meat.

NEFARIOUS HOLIDAY

I'm glad that it is Halloween.
Please hate me, because I'm obscene.
I know when, and I know why.
Enter my yard in order to die.

It's trick or treat.
You've come to eat.
There is a project;
I must complete.

I'm grateful that it's Halloween.
Let me show you what is obscene.
I put staples in your brand new candy.
It will only choke you;
It's fine and dandy.

It's Halloween.
You're painted green.
You have been seen.
It's Halloween.

Do you find Halloween extremely appealing?
A cream-filled treat with a skin-layered peeling.
Eat until you regurgitate, afterwards, eat more.
Lick the dirty sucker that you picked up off of the floor.

HEAVY PETTING

I'm the perfective one.
I want everything to remain clean.
My polish is vastly effective.
I refuse to refrain myself.

Heavy petting involved with contortions.
Heavy breeding with selective abortions.
I'm preparing my fists well for licking.
It's bizarre that your tongue isn't sticking.

You are not a perfective one.
You are nauseatingly dirty.
You're lacking in regard to standard cleanliness.
I'm without composure.

Heavy petting with dissolution.
Look at my self-inflicted contusion.
It works well because it's psychoactive.
I'm tired, but yet hyperactive.

EXPIRY

Observe my neoplasia.
There are always patterns to play with.
Study my reoccurring shakes.
Study my strange behavior.

I just found an ingrown object.
I'm preparing for my own interment.
Preparations for a first-rate burial.
My fever is shockingly malarial.

Undeserving of any sort of respect;
There's no doubt that you're a certified reject.
Immense undertakings that are worthwhile.
I'm indulging in my unhealthy lifestyle.

He's a leach of a human being.
He will never achieve well-being.
You're so small that you're physically distorted.
Your mother should have had you aborted.

EAT GLASS

Skipping class;
You missed the metaphor.
I don't genuinely care.
Life is such a whore.
By you, I'm not embraced.
By I, you are erased.
You missed the metaphor.
I am terribly sore.

Take one back to make it true.
You know that it's now even.
Cleanse one now to make it new.
Your mind is so uneven.

Eating glass;
It's good for trimming fat.
There's a window store.
You're exceptionally good at that.
It's evident you're dumb.
I'm evidence I'm glum.
Ripping your stomach lining;
Swallow, and stop your whining.

Move your mouth so you can chew.
It's appropriate for digestion.
We've decided to ballyhoo.
A perfect formula for indigestion.

BIRTHDAY SKULL

I am consistently deceiving.
You are fantastically relieving.
You should be proud of yourself.

I can't retrieve it.
You don't believe it.
You have wisely chosen to trick yourself.

I want to catch and spread disease.
There are new ones.
Infect me, will you, please?
Here's another one;
A skull for your birthday.
Just stay away from me, and I'll be okay.

My head is aching;
Suffering from an internal raking.
I keep her heart upon my shelf.

You are taking care of business.
You mind your own business.
I only contain her within myself.

I want to be stricken with disease.
There are many kinds.
Inject me, will you, please?
High tolerance with low endurance.
Thank you for your hopeless reassurance.

I'M ASTRAY

We are all out to purchase new arms.
They are all out to purchase new charms.
They went out to discover a new god.
We are all out to get a new fraud.

I am torn.
I am dead.
I'm alive.
I'm alive instead.

They all went to buy a better, new life.
We all went to buy a new strife.
They all spent their money much too soon.
Here comes someone else we can easily impugn.

I'm astray.
You're a stray.
You've been thrown;
Thrown away.

A SCIENCE EXAM ON A FRIDAY AFTERNOON

One more nephogram;
And we're home.
Here is a new exam;
Let's spit foam.
I just want to complete this;
And go home.
I just want to finish this;
And go roam.

A science exam.
A teacher's sacred lamb.
A teacher's scam.

One last nephogram;
And I'm sound.
Here is a new exam;
I'm unsound.
Let's just tear it up;
And leave school.
I myself choose to live;
Without rule.

Our science exam.
Our teacher's scam.
A sacrificial lamb.

ASPHYXIATION

She chose to asphyxiate herself.
He attempted to suffocate himself.
He gave up again to go sigh.
Unlike her, he failed to reach hypoxia.

Asphyxiation;
A new sensation.
Suffocation;
Permanent sedation.

Depression due to her suicide.
He promised to follow suit, but he lied.
This gun is for your mouth; open wide.
Another failure to commit suicide.

Don't disarm.
A body farm.
Interest in self-harm.
The fourth time is a charm.

He chose to asphyxiate himself;
Using some saran, and a belt.
He worked very hard to finally die.
He's finally achieved hypoxia.

A body bag;
With a signed toe tag.
Get a rag;
He's going stag.

LUCRATIVE SPENDING

I'm out of my mind.
Her lips are still, and never narrow.
What can I find?
I need to find whatever's costly.
I'm feeling the grind.
How much did the free item cost you?

Lucrative selling.
Lucrative mailing.
Lucrative telling.

You're inside my mind.
Her lips are red and never narrow.
What will we find?
I'm going to buy whatever's unhealthy.
I'm in a bind.
We'd like to take whatever's detrimental.

Lucrative spending.
Lucrative bending.
Lucrative ending.

SPITTING CLOVERS

March is finally back;
How about you?
I think that you have been altered.
If I do well;
Will you hate me?
My body has been altered.

Shades of green from splitting clovers.
Shades of green from spitting clovers.

I'm spewing well;
How about you?
I think you regurgitate clovers.
March is now here;
What I say is true.
Come and watch me vomit clovers.

Shades of green from counting clovers.
A tongue of green from spitting clovers.

INTRAVENOUS DRIPPINGS

I may have toxemia.
Shower me with your anodynes.
You know how to not mature well.
Lick your intravenous drippings.

My deterioration is persistent.
My faith is non-existent.
Your sister's face is intensely creepy.
I have no need for rest;
I'm not sleepy.

I might have toxemia.
Inject me with your anodynes.
You undoubtedly know how to nurture well.
Lick my intravenous drippings.

My demeanor is absolutely distant.
Gratification must always be instant.
Your mother is much too weepy.
I have no need for rest;
I am too sleepy.

DISFIGURATION

Everyone noticed his abnormality.
He couldn't manage his own reality.
I'm amused to say there's no cure for the broken.
I have ignored the words you have spoken.

Everyone made fun of his bodily form.
Beating him with sticks was the daily norm.
Saw off your legs to play kick the can.
Some species of rodents are the child of man.

Spoiled meat;
What a splendid treat.
Rotten flesh;
The scent is so fresh.

Count your blessings that you've been broiled.
It's evident that your flesh is spoiled.
Ashamed of his unusual, physical structure;
He prayed daily that his heart would rupture.

In the schoolyard, we would make him eat worms.
They provide protein and are ridden with germs.
When we finally murdered him it was no surprise.
We ripped out his veins as blood spewed from his eyes.

Decayed meat;
You are obsolete.
You'll be forgotten.
Go pick my cotton.

MOTHER'S MILK

You've been drinking your mother's milk.
Your mother's milk is as smooth as silk.
Reward her well, and, reward her often.
Put your best friend inside of a coffin.

It is gratifying to be nursed by the breast.
I'm being fed by her medicine chest.
She applies lotion to salvage each nipple.
With more effort, her production could triple.

I've been drinking your mother's milk.
Your mother's milk is as soft as silk.
It contains a lot of vitamin D.
She refuses to charge a fee.

They caught you drinking your mother's milk.
Mother's milk is as soothing as silk.
As of late, she has been reducing.
Drink it up before she stops producing.

NURTURING A DISEASE

I'm going to feed my disease.
I have to call one of my appointees.
Admire me for my discontent.
It continues to augment.

I am deeply in love with medication.
She didn't appreciate my desecration.
She became my obsession against her will.
I am lacking in regard to social skill.

Going to the same store repeatedly.
Leaving frustrated and departing heatedly.
Unlike I, she was sympathetic.
I've always viewed sympathy as extraordinarily pathetic.

She is by far my biggest fixation.
It's time to take my medication.
She was silent, in addition to, inwardly raging.
Her mom made her suffer by way of caging.

ORAL MALPRACTICE

Profiting from an acidic youth.
Let me jerk out your healthy tooth.
I always keep a pair of pliers near.
My treatment is gorgeously severe.

I have no experience in dentistry;
But in my chair is where you should be.
I am above while you are beneath.
Open up wide so I can yank out your teeth.

Profits from an obese youth.
I will start with an upper tooth.
You are not in need of any Novocain.
Stop complaining and enjoy the oral pain.

This is my first time performing dentistry.
Whoever said that you need to buy a degree?
This is a case of oral malpractice.
Go fetch your family; I need more practice.

ANOREXIC SANTA CLAUS

If you refuse to go to bed;
He will remove your head.
He vomits for a cause.
Anorexic Santa Claus.

Let him come into your home.
He wants to make you foam.
Delivering pain without a pause;
Is the anorexic Santa Claus.

Gagging is contagious;
Not to mention advantageous.
Puking without a pause;
Christmas' anorexic Santa Claus.

Your repellent scent tells him you are near.
His radar tells him when you are here.
He'll hate you if you act pleasant.
If you are pleasant you will not get a present.

Pestilence within finely wrapped boxes.
I want to see you open all of your boxes.
A self-appointed representative of Christ;
He releases more waste when he's enticed.

He only gives his best toys;
To the naughtiest girls and boys.
Go ahead, and hang your stocking.
Claus will soon be knocking.

He wants to beat you;
And maybe even eat you.
Afterwards, he'll throw-up.
He's posing for a close-up.

His stomach is churning.
He's internally burning.
Genocide without a pause;
The anorexic Santa Claus.

AGITATED ADOLESCENTS

Recognizing youth;
They've come to feel uncouth.
Beatings evermore;
The ones that moan are sore.
Take a look around.
Plant them in the ground.
Will they ever grow?
Will we ever know?

Agitated youth;
I'm glad you are uncouth.
You are used to scorn;
You moan because you're torn.
Try to get an E.
You can't count to three.
I know you'll get an F.
I think you're going def.

Agitated youth;
Never tell the truth.
Teachers teach you lies.
Don't study; improvise.
I'm beautifully addicted.
My reproduction tube is constricted.
Vicariously injected;
You have been infected.

GRASS CUTTER

He never makes decent money.
His allergies make his nose runny.
His mind stays in the gutter.
He is a grass cutter.

He's saving for some clothes.
His life really blows.
Maybe if, he slips;
The blade will cut off his toes.

He never bathes after he is done.
The grass itches when he stands in the sun.
His neighbors always made him nervous.
His neighbors devalued his service.

He cuts a lot of grass;
To stand out from the mass.
He's pinching pennies;
An investment in gas.

PERFIDIOUS PRIMATE

Juliana is waiting for her unworthy groom.
Your charity's not needed;
She uses her own broom.
She despises you due to your betrayal.
Another broken dream pissed in the urine well.

Perfidious human;
You are not human.
Deceitful primate;
You are an ingrate.

Juliana is serving her poisonous groom.
Your help is not needed;
She cleanses her own room.
She will always detest you because it's all your fault.
She'll use her eyes to turn you into a pillar of salt.

Duplicitous human;
You are inhuman.
Fraudulent primate;
Do not procreate.

INTERNALLY AFFLICTED

My temperature changed just as she predicted.
It's pleasant to be internally afflicted.
Worthless people are hard to endure.
I'm getting exposed to them more and more.

A new phase has arrived as was her prediction.
It's hard to abandon a satisfying addiction.
Here's what happened; isn't that a shame?
I am hostile, and you are fair game.

Ferociously bitter;
Because, the dull doesn't glitter.
It's unusually moist;
It's fun to foist.

I ripped out his vocal chords.
I should be given numerous awards.
Rest comes quicker now that he's a mute.
I'll make sure his pain stays acute.

Your no good name I will further defame.
He is one of many I'd like to maim.
Don't ask me for salvation.
I have a deeper interest in mutilation.

SEVERLY LIMITED SOCIAL RESOURCES

You will never receive any mercy from me.
I refuse your every plea.
I remain silent when I grit my teeth.
Syphilis upon a powdered wreath.

You will not receive a pardon from me.
I'm entertained by your desperate plea.
The deterioration of my health.
Eat my shit;
My shit has wealth.

Deterioration by my own hand.
I can only take as much as I can stand.
Here is another method of instigation.
An emblematic instance of irate desecration.

Shaking rapidly, because I'm constantly nervous.
You became prosperous from your valueless service.
A human waste-pan for bedside manners.
Advertising scabies by way of banners.

THE OBSTRUCTION OF THE OPPORTUNITY

There are many things to be said about the one who is regretful.
The regret of one thing in specific.
I feel terrific.
I'm being sarcastic.
A folded paper moistened by the snow.

She was accepting of the fact that the conversation wasn't pertaining.
At least she found it somewhat entertaining.
Moods are like billows.
I'm stabbing pillows.
An obstructed dream foiled by a lack of glow.

I should've discovered a way to guarantee my prompt arrival.
A strike of bad fortune.
A strike of misfortune.
This should have been reassembled years ago.

There are many things to be said about all who remain in a vicious cycle.
Nothing is changing.
It is deranging.
She's sad because her body's aching from head to toe.

TANGS

They're evolving where they lay.
They are constantly on display.
Habits difficult to break, and to sustain.
Maintain a steady diet of yellow rain.

Various people do various things.
I have a craving for many tangs.
I have forcibly altered your point of view.
There is no one more gullible than you.

Happiness is just a man-made myth.
Tell me what I have been stricken with.
All of the symptoms have been described.
I am taking what has been prescribed.

There is no antidote.
Patients taking this tend to bloat.
An irritating, common side-effect;
Induced by the pill with no effect.

SOUR STOMACH

There's a tightness inside my intestines.
Come and worship my tattered intestines.
Welcome to another miserable hour.
I am angry, and my stomach is sour.

Hemorrhoidal blood within my stool.
To me you're nothing more than a tool.
You and your kind I will always disdain.
When I spit in your face, it's your personal rain.

When it ruptures you will drool.
Let's go swimming in the toxic pool.
You are receiving what you are owed.
Your brain will now hemorrhage and then explode.

I'll persecute you for what you believe.
You're not trusted because you deceive.
It's time for you all to enter the shower.
I'm morally bankrupt, and my stomach is sour.

SERVITUDE

You have been begging for your savior.
You've bore witness to my manic behavior.
I despise you due to your nativity.
I'm the god of total negativity.

Servitude is your only beneficial feature.
Your mother gave birth to a horrible creature.
Your genetic properties have made you this way.
Physical properties are made to decay.

Seeing you starve is nurturing me.
You have never been good company.
Do you once more expect me to be your host?
It is your kind I loathe the most.

Now bear witness to my manic impulsions.
Watch me go into violent convulsions.
I want to destroy your nativity.
You've indulged in my creativity.

AVANT-GARDE PRODUCTION

A lot of new things to discard;
Worthless people are thrown away.
What I write is avant-garde.
Sweat drips due to my dismay.

Sunny days filled with despair;
Urinary tract beyond repair.
Interred behind a wall of bricks;
You are one I will transfix.

A lot of things to disregard.
I just wish you'd disappear.
All I create is avant-garde.
All you do is interfere.

Transfix;
A crucifix.
I am thorough.
You dwell within a burrow.

PROPERLY PRUNED

Salt rests best within an open wound.
Rotten fruits even though the plant was properly pruned.
I didn't get any rest today.
Sleeping is without closure anyway.

I just can't get over her.
Smoke makes life feel like a blur.
Pupils dilated from pupil deeds.
Tightly compressed with a lot of seeds.

Undertaking tasks is what I should do.
Physical labor makes me want to spew.
I prefer to work within deep thought.
Highly unstable and self-taught.

I don't want to get over her.
My situation I did incur.
Wallowing in a state of misery.
Self-induced, inward injury.

SATISFACTION DERIVED FROM THE EXTRACTION

Lying comfortably upon a bed of nails.
A nail per every inch never fails.
Roles fulfilled, and primates reversed.
They entered my chamber without being coerced.

Handcuffed to the bedpost of despair.
For you, I will never care.
Take advantage of rather than nurture.
A heavy inquiry wearing searcher.

There are many skeletons within the closet of truth.
The ripping out of your healthy tooth.
Prepare in detail for the extraction.
The result is from the contraction.

What I have, and what I've had.
Unwell emotions aren't so bad.
An extreme, non-mutual attraction.
Obvious is my dissatisfaction.

SALIVATE

I want it.
I want it all.
Let them fall as they squall.

It's another period.
Another period of tedium.
You're of boring quality.
I think I'll buy a medium.

Making profound statements.
I'm one of the patients.
Withstanding the waiting room.
I like it here I assume.

I want them;
I want them all.
It is fun to appall.

You should remain stationary.
The underling's probationary.
Soon I will fire him.
He loves to lick his phantom limb.

I'm basking in the current gloom.
I like it here I presume.
A prescription elevation;
With no alleviation.

I need her.
I need her all.
She wouldn't take my phone call.

KAPOSI'S SARCOMA

It's been many years since Charlie has showered.
By a rapist, he was roughly deflowered.
Born a piece of trash, he will remain the same.
Generations of incest are most likely to blame.

He wears a dress because he's a homosexual.
The frigid turnip has become hypersexual.
Charlie was placed in a nursing home.
He acquired immune deficiency syndrome.

He's such a mess.
His stature is small.
Refuse to feed him.
Don't feed him at all.

Transfusion trades;
He's learned a trade.
Spread it on purpose;
Another one laid.

Partaking in the spreading of Aids.
Sharing blood by way of needles and razor blades.
I enjoy seeing his many defections.
He has lost the ability to fight infections.

He's expecting to die from pneumonia;
Either that, or Kaposi's Sarcoma.
His request was to be cremated.
Instead, for him a black casket awaited.

Infect them with;
Immune system disease.
There is no cure.
Spread and seize.

Sniff really hard.
Smell the aroma.
Charlie died;
From Kaposi's Sarcoma.

BITTER PEA

I refuse to get your consent.
You're one of many that I resent.
Your permission is something that I don't need.
The enjoyment of a fine misdeed.

The current situation is unacceptable.
Things that are obvious are perceptible.
Your lack of loyalty was well perceived.
The best pains are ones that can't be relieved.

I live my life bitterly.
Yes, I mean that literally.
I do everything for my own sake.
What you have is for me to take.

You're not entitled to ownership.
I'd love to beat you with a whip.
A great performance deserves applause.
Lick my collection of dirty gauze.

Practice chain smoking every day.
We all die eventually anyway.
Always do what I recommend.
Heed to every word that I have penned.

She spit out a bitter pea.
I have of her, but a memory.
We put gum in his nappy hair.
He's a nasty subhuman I do declare.

INTERNAL ORGANS

All of the best fruits are forbidden.
Rest assured that your secrets won't remain hidden.
You must come to the realization;
The reality of this manifestation.

You must come to this realization.
Persecution and masturbation.
Do you like the pleasant taste?
Your life has been such a waste.

I indulged in the infestation.
I enjoyed the manifestation.
Your suffering makes my pain lessen.
I'm removing your organs to teach you a lesson.

You must think that you are something special.
I know that I am especial.
Many people rest in excretion.
Let me live inside your wet secretion.

I am greatly enhanced by physical perfection.
Obvious is my predilection.
Virtuousness is not our obligation.
Morality is just an aggravation.

EXTERNAL ORGANS

You are a selected individual.
I take pleasure in the mutilation ritual.
The sensation is much better when you don't forgive.
All of the painful memories you must relive.

Be grateful for being a chosen individual.
The damage that I do to you will be visual.
I'll treat you like an object, not a person.
Squirm as I cut, so your pain will worsen.

I must make sure that you are feeling this.
How about I seal your fate as you reminisce?
First removing all of your parts, which are external.
I do my work at night because I am nocturnal.

You're tonight's selected individual.
You will be subjected to my mutilation ritual.
It is always more fun when you are the giver.
A butchered corpse carried to shore by the river.

ORGANS: (BOTH INTERNAL AND EXTERNAL)

It's just too simple to see.
I sense you inside of me.
It is exceedingly easy you see?
Love's living well with sodomy.

You are my subject to be.
Committing the act of sodomy.
Approach me now, my victim to be.
I am without sympathy.

Degeneration due to lack of use.
To some the meaning is abstruse.
Infatuated with her to the highest degree.
Love coincides with sodomy.

WORM

He is a minute, unimpressive worm.
Witness his uncoordinated squirm.
He is inconsequential, as well as, complacent.
The dampest soil is adjacent.

Being injured within;
He's in a pen.
Damaged long-term;
He is a worm.

He remains disgusting and slimy.
He is one of many that I must stymie.
You're a piece of valueless human bait.
A reduction in significance; you always deflate.

The hindrance of progress.
He hinders the process.
You're obstructionistic.
Now you're a statistic.

WORM: (MEGADRILE)

Positioned upon a bed of nails.
I have been collecting snails.
Despite the foul odor, I'm not removing the body.
He was embarrassed because his clothing was gaudy.

Earthworm or megadrile.
Release my yellow bile.
Slither to me, worm.
I'm damaged long-term.

The obstruction of progress.
You are causing my distress.
I want to be far away from you.
Do you see what you have put me through?

Earthworm or megadrile.
His efforts are so futile.
The losing of vitality.
An escape from reality.

It is complacent.
Moist soil's adjacent.
Dig your tunnel.
The surface is fungal.
Study it's squirm.
Observe the worm.

WORM: (CESTOIDEA)

What is it like being a hermaphrodite?
You are someone they can not disinvite.
They all have a special interest.
They are amazed by your disinterest.

They really want to study your species.
They have an urge to examine your feces.
I've decided to treat you like an object.
It produces a cognitive effect.

Cestoidea;
Euphoria.
Parasitic flatworms;
That suck life on their own terms.

Cestoidea;
Euphoria.
Parasitic tapeworms;
They suck life on their own terms.

WORM: (TAENIA SOLIUM)

Your tapeworm is living off of you.
I've created a situation that I can't undo.
Taenia Soliums are hermaphrodites.
You have attempted to cover up your human bites.

What is it like being one's definitive host?
Which sensation makes you suffer the most?
It is devouring you on the inside.
The tapeworm is nurtured by what you provide.

A scolex attached to your intestine.
You've always been unable to predestine.
You're undeserving of every gift that you've received.
I'm delighted that he was one that I aggrieved.

You've earned every bit of pain that you've received.
Your insignificance is not to be believed.
I'm doing what I can to make his death more painful.
Such acts are gratifying, as well as, gainful.

What is it like being a hermaphrodite?
You are someone they can't disinvite.
They all have a special interest.
They're amazed by your disinterest.

Cestoidea;
Euphoria.
Parasitic tapeworms;
They suck life on their own terms.

Cestoidea;
Euphoria.
Parasitic flatworms;
That suck life on their own terms.

They really want to study your species.
They have an overwhelming urge to examine your feces.
I have decided to treat you like an object.
It produces a cognitive effect.

Cestoidea;
Phantasmagoria.
You're a parasitic flatworm.
Your attachment remains firm.

Cestoidea;
Phantasmagoria.
You're a parasitic tapeworm.
Your organism is infirm.

Are you angry that you're not treated right?
Before you, his skin cells were fed on by larval mites.
You're located in the host's small intestine.
This is the Cestoidea resurrection.

THE PLEASURE OF VENGENCE

He's been known to experience kleptophilia.
Donate your feces to contribute to his coprophilia.
He smells inexistent odors, because of phantosmia.
You don't recognize the name, due to your anomia.

Your head I will now impinge.
Here is my pleasurable revenge.
I am the one that you unhinged.
Now my damage is avenged.

A blood ridden body wrapped in a white sheet.
You are another object to mistreat.
I have become what you knew I'd be.
I am Satan; come and worship me.

Did you enjoy that twinge?
I get off when you cringe.
On your pain, I binged.
Your face I singed.

Sacred is the serial killer's ritual.
Such criminality is habitual.
A number of us choose to devour.
Violence never fails to empower.

Your head I impinged.
Yes, I'm unhinged.
Sweet was my revenge.
Laws you must infringe.

I have been avenged.
Laws I've infringed;
On flesh we'll binge;
Obtaining revenge.

I have been unfairly disrespected.
By society, I remain rejected.
I am not even suspected.
A propensity to be creative.
The results are always probative.

Casual comments are atypical.
I find that you're somewhat hypocritical.
I'm secretive and well mannered.
Hold me to a high standard.
I am a serial killer.

His natural being is not typical.
You're stereotypical.
He's outwardly polite.
I hunt for people at night.
I am a serial killer.

Cutting up humans is tantalizing.
Tearing up the human body is hypnotizing.
I'm continuing to butcher while analyzing.
Such a fine activity is to be admired.
There are many more that remain desired.

Admire the way, I rip up the bodies.
I'm the character your child embodies.
Telephones greatly rattle my nerves.
My first victim had impressive curves.
I am a serial killer.

I'm comfortable with my identity.
Tearing flesh provides serenity.
Some find my actions appalling.
I wonder what they'll do when I come calling.
I am a serial killer.

Now I am respected.
To my wrath you were subjected.
Continuing to be socially rejected.
I have been excluded.
My beautiful work could not have been precluded.

VISCERA EXPOSURE

The most violent brain; a therapist's enigma.
We are all subject to stigma.
I torture him because I don't respect him.
You cannot be saved by any prayer or hymn.

Pure exposure;
With full enclosure.
Complete exposure;
Combined with full disclosure.

Practice makes for absolute, oral perfection.
It is senseless to wear sexual protection.
A new reality to observe the old one.
The present tense, and the purchase of a new gun.

I cannot find closure.
Who needs composure?
An inability to sleep at night.
Yes, I am uptight.

Everything's costly, and nothing's for free.
I want you to place the blame upon me.
I'm brainwashing the minds of all beneath.
I am the granter of the lashing of teeth.

Pure exposure;
Whipping within the enclosure.
Viscera exposure;
I've lost my composure.

Viscera exposure;
Within the enclosure.
Intestine exposure;
I have no composure.

NO EXCULPATION

Schoolyard beatings;
The all-American birth right.
Sometimes the abusers get beat.
I ravage you;
It's my fucking birth right.
I am going to split you in two.

Do not forgive.
Do not forget.
They will be subjected.
They will feel pain yet.

Some believe in reincarnation;
But then again most people are fools.
I believe in your pretty castration.
You have disobeyed my rules.

No room for exculpation.
No tolerance for compassion.
Extermination;
In the most brutal fashion.

Public disgrace and humiliation.
It is due to your peers.
Public disgrace and public castration.
It has been effective for years.

Do not pardon.
Show no mercy.
Possessing an enemy's corpse.
Let it harden.

A COLLECTION OF MANNEQUINS

A field full of fabulous mannequins.
You are fake just like my mannequins.
Don't you think that they are looking good?
I am violent and anti-brotherhood.

Look at all of the stupid individuals.
They are missing obvious signals.
They can't discover the host with the most.
You provide nothing, yet you boast.

My collection of mannequins;
You know that they are beauteous.
I dressed up my mannequins.
The project was studious.

Flagrant people are somewhat like me;
Scandalous, but to a lesser degree.
My mannequins; I have fixed them up real pretty.
Remove your face, because you look shitty.

An introduction to my mannequins;
They have described all that they've withstood.
You want to play with my mannequins.
The reasoning behind this is that they make you feel good.

It's time to collect.
It is time to collect humans.
You must die;
You are subhuman.

JUDAS TREE

Those that I choose to make fall;
I'll dismember their bodies with a saw.
I'm indulging in my surgical gown.
Happy is he who wears the crown.

It looks like you have not been blessed.
You will die because you, I detest.
Quickly they are losing girth.
I'm the Satan of mother fucking earth.

Mass starvation;
In my genocide nation.
Privations;
With amputations.

Incarceration;
There's no lactation.
Deprivation;
To strengthen my nation.

Use your tongue to clean up the afterbirth.
I'm the Lucifer upon the earth.
Burn what is sacrosanct to you now.
To me you will forever bow.

If, in I, you display any doubt.
I will personally snuff you out.
If you decide to disagree;
I'll hang your eyes from a Judas tree.

ANTISOCIAL BUTTERFLY

Antisocial butterfly;
An increase in moodiness when it's dry.
I've been thinking of many things.
Perfect consistency with battered wings.

Antisocial butterfly;
Amassing your type was worth a try.
You have come to realize what I can do.
Avoidance objectives to pursue.

Avoiding social gatherings.
Not caring what tomorrow brings.
A residential admission fee.
Not interacting with the community.

Staying away from the other residents.
Setting a fresh, antisocial precedence.
It's the new standard of non-communication.
She is pleased with the causation.

Antisocial Butterfly;
I will pull your wings, so you will sigh.
I'm going to limit the activities that you can do.
Tear them off, and then imbue.

Antisocial Butterfly;
I'll spit on them before I die.
You and I have a lot in common.
Our behaviors are superlatively uncommon.

BRAINWASH

The value of what is not sentimental.
Don't follow the guidance that is parental.
Like a puppet I will pull your strings.
You are all my dysfunctional playthings.

Cover your own mouth with duck tape.
This is an instance of psychological rape.
Practice the method that always works.
Destroying yourself has it's perks.

Here's a picture of what I used to be.
My bedroom is currently filled with debris.
Most criminals start with vandalism.
Let yourself be drawn in by evil's magnetism.

Don't allow yourself to be misrepresented.
All human beings are perverse and demented.
Don't flatter yourself; you never were charming.
Your only value is that you are worth harming.

Go slay your fellow man, because it feels good.
Do as I say just as you should.
Drinking gasoline surely stings.
Your minds are my tiny playthings.

TRUE FLAVORS

I am pleased to know that you are so far able.
I suspect that you realize that I'm unstable.
You have given to me a new assortment of rapid flavors.
You've supplied for me a numerous amount of true favors.

There is no one around.
There are chalk drawings upon the ground.
I'll pick flowers for you.
Your favorite color is blue.
Allow me to push the swing.
My heart is in a sling.
My eternal you;
Your saliva tastes brand new.

You will be amused when you think about what I have been missing.
I am the most deeply amused when my penis stings while I'm pissing.
You're certainly the appropriate mate because you're not imprudent.
The emotional lines that we draw are well defined and so congruent.

There's no one around.
You are the one that I've found.
Tasting flavors of lipstick.
You are my clock's eternal tick.
Let me run my fingers through your dark hair.
You're unequivocally debonair.
My eternal you;
The flavors of your tongue are true.

DOUBLE STANDARD

You're leaving now because the conversation's so good.
Gossip is maintaining.
Some are misunderstood.
They don't know what they're even talking about.
An ounce of respect;
That's something they live without.

Things are not always what they may seem.
At least within her life;
There's some type of theme.
That's more than I can say about yours.
Follow your instincts;
Stand on all fours.

If she was a man they would glorify her score;
But since she's a girl;
She's labeled a whore.
That's what I call the obvious double standard.
It just may be the case;
That her character's been slandered.

She doesn't care what they have to say.
Her instincts tell her;
To go her own way.
They have no vision because they cannot see.
I'm going to follow her example;
And start living for me.

CASTRATION

Energized by a constant fixation;
It is time for your pretty castration.
I've always been one who entices.
I'm not in total control of my own devices.

You will never have the ability to provide.
What is certain you cannot hide.
There isn't a need for a demonstration.
The use of garden shears for your castration.

Castration;
Prior to lactation.
I heard a ting.
Prevent the birth of his offspring.

As a result of the reduction;
You're now incapable of reproduction.
Separate yourself from others to become a recluse.
People like you shouldn't reproduce.

It's so funny to look at you now.
You are losing blood quickly, and you're hung like a cow.
Did you enjoy your total genitalia castration?
She received artificial insemination.

Castration;
A forced alteration.
He has been torn;
Fewer infrahumans born.

PUTREFACTION

What's wrong with you; you don't appear normal?
Wear your worst clothes, because the dinner is formal.
He tried every method to spread his seed.
He attempted many times, but he could not breed.

Set out the meat, and allow it to spoil.
I've been smoking my dope on aluminum foil.
The compulsive one is compulsively vain.
I am proud of my abdominal strain.

Confidence without a sense of hope.
An innate inability to cope.
Dizziness combined with numbness from the panic.
Everything is fine now that I have turned manic.

I love hate, in addition to, sin.
Garbage like you belongs in a bin.
I abuse myself well, and also often.
I will find relief in a red-carpeted coffin.

OBEDIENT, HUMAN EXCRETAL RAG

Whether you believe it or not you are expendable.
I cannot depend on you because you're not dependable.
Exploring many avenues in search of reliance.
You should display to me your absolute compliance.

Surrender, and yield your independence to me.
My subservient slave is what you should be.
I prefer it immensely when you are obedient;
But I'll beat you anyway because I'm not lenient.

Lick up the liquid I have spilt.
Expect no mercy; I'm incapable of feeling guilt.
I am one who will forever hold a grudge.
God only created you for me to judge.

I am comfortable with this current arrangement.
Perhaps it is in part due to my estrangement.
On your behalf, no one will advocate.
I've taken your individuality; it's too late.

COGNIZANCE, IN ADDITION TO, ATTENTION TO DETAIL

I'm going to thoroughly read your diary.
I want to know your private, personal thoughts.
What is it that you have been writing about?
She has a forbidden, hidden text.

Nothing is sacred anymore.
Someone told me that you kept it in the top drawer.
Within the top drawer of your busted chest.
My emotions remain repressed.
Every day of your miserable life is described.
By me, every single word has been imbibed.
By society everyone's molested.
My soul remains infested.

Allow me to read your diary.
I want to live inside of you.
She's the one I want to be the most cognizant of.
She's the one that I want to be the most familiar with.

Eating feces provides a special odor.
It's written in plain text; you don't need a decoder.
The excitement of lacerating.
Degrading others I find personally aiding.
The preciousness of infliction.
Stress related throat constriction.
A decrease in circulatory activity.
My pessimistic proclivity.

Her diary was very insightful.
Her diary was extremely good.
It contained a lot of information.
I'm glad that I have accumulated knowledge of her insight.

It's satisfying to realize her point of view.
I'm happy that I know what she's thinking about.
Maybe I can use it to my advantage.
With her, I want to engage in acts of intimacy.

EXTANT

I can't afford anything because I am broke.
On your pork, I'll watch you choke.
None of my statements will undergo retraction.
I could care less about your reaction.

You don't mean anything to me.
You're as important as an absentee.
Destroy your own residence.
I am setting a new precedence.

Do with me what you will.
Empty once not to refill.
A social security disability check.
It isn't much; it's just a speck.

A purposely induced stagflation.
The removal of the foundation.
Look terribly hard to find the obvious source.
Persist in your failure to maintain the course.

Ask yourself why you are here?
It is easy to disappear.
Angular distance measured with a sextant.
You certainly shouldn't be extant.

THE MAIDEN'S GARDEN

Beyond the gates lies the Maiden's garden.
The flies are dead; allow them to harden.
She lashed you because you're provoking.
The Maiden enjoys her chain smoking.

I want to rest within the Maiden's comfortable garden.
I want to lie, and lie to you within the Maiden's garden.
There's no doubt that I will enjoy my stay here.
The Maiden is merciless, and she has such a keen ear.

We will practice various techniques to increase the torment.
That technique is reflective of a personal ferment.
She will never grant you a pardon.
You'll remain in the Maiden's garden.

We will most certainly torture you.
Even your soft whispers she can construe.
No protection; nothing for buffering.
We will revel in your suffering.

PERSONAL PROPERTY

Wear this collar around your neck.
You are my perfect wreck.
Tie this knot around your soul.
I want to maintain complete control.

This is a power grab.
The structure is prefab.
My institution has a reason.
You have committed treason.

I do not remit.
To I, you must submit.
You live in squalor.
You're growing paler in color.

A dominant exhibition.
I have put you in this condition.
You only exist to be dominated.
By I, you have been incarcerated.

How do you like your chain?
Authority I must maintain.
Eat from your dirty bowl.
Your master you must extol.

You are what I've created.
Your spirit has been deflated.
My slave is a moaner.
I am your owner.

FOR THE IMPRESSIONABLE READER

You should vomit everything that you eat.
It will keep you physically obsolete.
He decided to perform an act of incest.
He's been drinking from Lucifer's breast.

Nurture me with your scorn.
I am glad that your child is torn.
You won't find mercy here.
I will provide for you what is severe.

You are a certified prick.
The very sight of you makes me sick.
I want you to crawl, as well as, be servile.
Tip up your glass, and finish your bile.

Play with your daddy's gun.
You know that daddy wants you to have fun.
Put it up to your head.
You are not a thoroughbred.

Throw yourself away.
I'll watch you decay.
You're one of his mistakes.
Look at how many he makes.

Blow yourself away.
Dismay.
I will give you encouragement;
For your discouragement.

HEMISECTION

Once was lost, and still not found.
Remember the statements that are profound.
None of us are granted impunity.
Is someone doing this to punish me?

Punish me for what I have done.
Make a label for each one.
Every single action that you can name.
You are not perfect you're just perfectly lame.

I don't owe anything to you.
Thanks to your assistance I did not accrue.
Wipe your feet on my unwelcome mat.
Come on in; I am up at-bat.

You lack any sort of intellect.
Your body I'm going to hemisect.
I have long awaited this bisection.
You're the latest addition to my garbage collection.

SELF-MUTILATION WHORE

He is the masturbation whore.
He enjoys playing with himself.
He doesn't have anyone to mingle with.
A product of odd positioning.

A spermatozoon detector for detection.
The unstable person's stable erection.
They want you to take notice of his disfiguration.
Deprived of a limb, by way of mutilation.

Rapid eye movements even when you're awake.
Did you enjoy your dead cousin's wake?
At the front door, they handed out the program.
It was planned well;
They finally hit a grand slam.

He is the self-mutilation whore.
Cutting without healing has served him well.
Interferences within the process.
Personal obstacles that he cannot overcome.

PUTRESCENCE WITHIN THE PROXIMITY

Here are the bodies; They're ready to burn.
You receive everything that you do not earn.
You are going to get exactly what you deserve.
Valueless objects are what you conserve.

He needs more than he is going to get.
In your blemished face, I spit.
He is exactly what he didn't want to be.
Putrescence within the proximity.

His hair's full of lice.
Isn't that nice?
What does it mean?
He is not clean.

He always did everything that everyone else insisted.
I took many different medications, but the problem persisted.
I abuse caffeine to stay awake.
It's perfectly normal to jerk and shake.

He always claimed that optimism once had existed.
He did what they told him and never resisted.
He's very much into taking orders.
In order to get filthy, he began dwelling with hoarders.

His hair's full of lice.
Isn't it nice?
He's a worthless whore.
He's very sore.

I will advance because I am not giving.
He will regress because he is forgiving.
He is exactly where he didn't want to be.
Putrescence within the proximity.

Yourself you should erase.
Spray yourself with mace.
He's still poor.
He'll never be more.

CARREN'S BEAUTEOUSNESS AND INTELLECT

Carren knows where Carren goes.
She isn't worried about the safety.
Look through your painted windows.
I might do that tomorrow; Maybe.

Carren grows what Carren sows.
She is never lazy.
The majority of people are shit.
I hope she doesn't blame me.

Patrick's still a reject.
Soon I'll be unconscious.
For the merciful man, I have no respect.
I'm glad that I'm obnoxious.

What Carren wants she's going to get.
I'm going to make sure that it happens.
She's beautiful and legit.
I'm genuinely glad that this happened.

Carren knows about my habits.
I do not nurture my body.
Bear witness to my sabbats.
I do it to disembody.

PESTILENTIAL CONTAINMENT

How it does spread, that what is contagious.
A transmissible disease.
I must protect her from what is contagious.
My mind is not at ease.

Your containment;
Let's frame it.
Your suffering is my entertainment.
Your imprisonment;
It's for my own good.
I'm going to do this just as I should.

I must guard her from all that is disadvantageous.
Embrace all which is demonic.
Mesmerized by what is contagious.
I am pleased that his pain is chronic.

I strain.
You're contained.
Your malnourishment is well maintained.
The portrait;
It's been framed.
The portrait showing that you I've maimed.

They have discovered that the latest plague is, in fact, pneumonic.
Engage in practices that are demonic.
The physically deformed child's spiteful reply was well done and laconic.
It's comforting to know that his pain is chronic.

Wheel chair bound with no aspirations;
He has no desire to achieve.
He has run out of anticipations.
Despite death, his pain will not leave.

                          .

My whip;
Your lashing.
To tear your flesh was beautifully smashing.
It's eating you;
Your ailment.
I'm preparing a stake for your impalement.

INTROVERT

I have difficulty making some decisions;
Even if they seem simple enough.
Vision and mass idea collisions.
Things are staying somewhat rough.

I hate you for what you have obtained.
I'm not at ease because I am strained.
My life is lacking spontaneity.
Between the couple, there's no homogeneity.

Do I just think this due to my jealousy?
I have been trying zealously.
I'm trying to find a female of my own.
How this works, remains unknown.

I am withdrawn, and I'm confused.
The in person option was misused.
The difficulty that does maintain.
Ignore the provisions I can't sustain.

I can't provide for you what you need.
Despite this fact, do not recede.
To her the situation is new.
Providing her with more facts is overdue.

DADDY'S LITTLE SPOILER

I unquestionably need a wife;
A personal life.
I could use some relief.
Stab me with a knife.

Daddy's little spoiler;
He gets in the way.
He pleas for attention.
He wants it all day.

I wish we would have had a girl.
I wish I had a daughter.
I'll get rid of this little boy.
He will be the first one I slaughter.

Daddy's little spoiler;
You're going to go in the boiler.
I refuse to conserve.
We get what we deserve.

Daddy's little spoiler;
Why won't you go away?
You never listen;
To what I say.

The plan is spoiled.
He spoils everything.
I haven't gotten my pearl.
Why couldn't we have had a girl?

SCRAPE MUFFIN

Scrape Muffin;
She smokes in the bathroom.
In her spare time;
She's running the vacuum.
I'm beginning to bloat.
Let her cut your throat.
I like the clothes you wear.
Let's share the things we tear.

Scrape Muffin;
Don't allow your skin to roughen.
He caused all of your scrapes.
I'm going to use his skin for drapes.

I'll transfix him with a pole.
I'm out of control.
Transfixion; amputating a limb.
I can't believe you were going to marry him.

Many people; have no taste, or vision.
His discarding of you was his most foolish decision.
Let me see you twirl.
You're a gorgeous girl.

Scrape Muffin;
You're everything to me.
I love everything about you;
Let's share our misery.
Feed off of me.
I refuse to flee.
Preciously wounded;
We're both so wounded.

IN REFERENCE TO AN UNNAMED INDIVIDUAL

You have fallen for the oldest trick within the oldest book.
Beads of sweat are rolling down your head as everyone takes a look.

He's wiping down the halls.
He talks to the walls.
Yeah, he's his own best friend.
He has many pet peeves.
He sees signs within the leaves.
I don't have an extra hand to lend.

I have learned how gullible you are.
Of yourself, you should be ashamed.
Your parents knew for sure that you would amount to nothing;
That is why you remain unnamed.

He isn't steady, nor is he ready for what the next day will bring.
To his imaginary friends he will undoubtedly cling.

He couldn't get what he was searching for, so he had to make a pact.
Mr. Welcome Ear, isn't welcome here;
He's been attempting to attract.
I recommend wearing cologne;
You'll never be grown.
Isolation is just a fact.

He tried to go outside to no avail.
He got lost in his own back yard.
It justifies embarrassment;
They continue to worship lard.

EXPIRATION DATE

You are going to expire at your current age.
You have now reached your life's final stage.
The subject has been humiliated, as well as, denuded.
I'm thirsty for food and hungry for fluid.

A worthless wasted youth for sale.
I am utterly sick, and I am pale.
Various types of emotional pain.
More semen down the semen drain.

Upon the grasses of the earth;
They all bore witness to a stillbirth.
You deserve to die; it is obvious that you do.
I am going to emasculate you.

You do not glitter.
I'll prevent your litter.
Emasculation;
No insemination.

I am so bitter.
I must thwart your litter.
I tend to scowl.
You, I'll disembowel.

HIGH PRESSURE SITUATIONS

There are many high pressure situations.
Blood pressure, and heart rate numbing sensations.
It is difficult to go to the grocery store.
I have had plenty; give me some more.

They spotted him stealing bananas.
He conceals his identity using bandanas.
The store can no longer sell them at a discounted price.
His shoplifting methodology was precise.

They are in dire need of new management.
I'm well aware of my psychological mismanagement.
Using his tongue, the subject mopped the floor.
The degradation of others is something I adore.

Let me mention something, you ugly cashier;
This is your life sentence; that is by far your biggest fear.
He is praying for death at this stage.
He gives his plasma for under minimum wage.

A dreadful beginning to a miserable day.
My nerves aren't behaving in a proper way.
Tension, as well as, tingling sensations.
Approaching is more high pressure situations.

I turn everything into a serious deal.
Your fine service was not genteel.
Suffocate the little boy with a bag made of plastic.
Elimination is natural and fantastic.

MASS EXTERMINATION

You're one of many I want to eliminate.
It is fun to eradicate.
Always shatter the first glass that spills.
Extermination using various skills.

I'm not an individual whom imitates.
I am one who violates.
It is you, in addition to many others, I want to irritate.
Here is your zero-dollar rebate.

Deception spreads easily, as does chickenpox.
Let me store your entrails in a box.
I have always been the type of person who likes to discredit.
I once owned a pet human but never fed it.

Reoccurring panic with disorientation.
You will now undergo acidification.
Are you smart, or do you think I care?
You're unintelligent and unaware.

COMPOSURE BY WAY OF EXPOSURE

Placed within the unwanted section.
You better line up for selection.
I find it amusing that you are conceited.
I prefer not to be greeted.

My most feeble of glands has secreted.
I am angry because I have been cheated.
Come and see my nicotine stain collection.
Nothing says happy like an infection.

Partaking in acts of self-medication.
The failure to achieve insemination.
Notice my unwillingness to agree.
Shunned, and ignored was the detainee.

She exposed them all to her radiation.
She exposed them all without hesitation.
I will find comfort through constant exposure.
A stimulant rests within losing composure.

ANTAGONISM

Your overall value is really thin.
I just insulted you with my pen.
Collect previously chewed chewing gum.
You've been discarded, because you are scum.

I always have a need.
Do not intercede.
Keep the friction in place.
We always have a need.
You shouldn't be freed.
You can't maintain the pace.

I don't know why she loves him instead of me.
She must be fond of abuse and misery.
He's an inadequate convenience store cashier.
Superglue on your skin will adhere.

I don't have what I need.
They always intercede.
You keep the tension in place.
You have everything you need.
I puncture to bleed.
You're not moving apace.

PSYCHOLOGICAL RAPE

I am plotting.
He can shit without squatting.
You can't save me;
I'm so distressed.
Cardboard is hard to digest.

Extreme pain with no reaction.
Bodily harm will keep you in shape.
Achievements with no satisfaction.
Teachers practicing psychological rape.

I am rotting.
She is excellent at trotting.
Assist me;
I really need resuscitation.
I'm preparing for my final ejaculation.

A discharge from the pleasure zone.
A favorable result just as I'd anticipated.
Taking a hammer to your occipital bone.
It comforts me that we are not related.

Continuous actuality.
Test it's lethality.
Investigate the alternatives;
The other choices.
Listen to your naughty mental voices.

An emission from my bitter soul.
The total destruction of everyone with a certain look.
You'll learn more techniques when you enroll.
I've obtained another individual for my meat hook.

NECROPHILIAC

He needs to find more corpses for sex.
He is the victim of an everlasting hex.
It's hard to find someone out there;
Of this fact, he's all too aware.

For him, nothing ever turns out right.
He's been going to the graveyard every night.
He get's the freshest corpses he can.
After all, he's a picky man.

He originally discovered what he was in a tome.
After he digs them up he takes his lovers home.
Living all alone;
Allows his secret to remain unknown.

Life has torn his mind asunder.
What he needs is six-feet under.
In his van, he carries a large black sack.
He is a necrophiliac.

To our kind boy the world has been giving.
Now he is taking into his possession the living.
First he dissects;
Then he uses their lifeless bodies for sex.

EXOTIC NEUROTIC

Enter into my misery chamber;
I'm without relief.
Follow me into my beauty chamber;
The pain is beyond belief.

I'm mean.
You're nice;
Pent-up like Jesus Christ.
You're lean.
I demean.
He's perspiring his saline.

Formulate a new concoction.
Prepare your tonic.
Sell your soul at an auction.
The gore is Messianic.

You've been priced.
I'm sliced;
Crucified like Jesus Christ.
Malcontent;
I'm spent.
Full of scorn and discontent.

I've created the perfect setting.
There are many to persecute.
I want you to find me besetting.
My vast, vaginal pursuit.

I am diced.
Wood spliced.
Crucified like Jesus Christ.
I deceive.
You grieve.
Suffering is without reprieve.

Cleanse your skin with a toxic toner.
Don't nurture your property.
You've been speaking to your blood donor.
Problems relative to neuropathy.

You're acquiescent.
You've been sent.
You were made obedient.
He is not;
My owner.
He is just your blood donor.

DEJECTION TURNED INTO ERADICATION

I always want what I can't have.
My heart is hers to halve.
Take it all before you leave me.
Is this the way life is supposed to be?

The prevalence of my absolute madness.
It is maintained by my sadness.
It's not my fault, so don't blame me.
I cannot find a sense of inner harmony.

Human life starts as a cum wad.
Sometimes I question the existence of god.
Shake and pound once you awaken.
The chosen rats have been forsaken.

I could care less about your views.
One of the places you'll see me is on the news.
I have gained knowledge from personal experience and history.
My tongue is very blistery.

Your insides are so synthetic.
Give me a boost to make me energetic.
I'd like to finish the job I've started.
Let's all urinate on the departed.

PERPETUAL ILLNESS

Looking at your perpetual illness.
Your skin is red.
Staring at your perpetual illness.
Your skin is dead.

Crucifixions near mortuaries;
They are so conveniently arranged.
Crucifixes by mortuaries;
I am exceedingly impressed, as well as, deranged.

You're ill.
You're still.
Do you save the skin that you peel?
His faced changed.
It's ashen.
We're from a god with no compassion.

Has your family prepared for the burial?
The time is drawing near.
I hear your dad's work is actuarial.
Your condition is severe.

You're sick.
I tick.
The flakes must itch; that's why you pick.
Your adherence.
Your appearance.
Within you must lie perseverance.

Alteration;
An explanation.
Have you thought about cremation?
A red coffin.
The deal is Faustian.
A minuscule coffin for your exhaustion.

TERRIFICALLY TART

I just wonder if you forgot.
Forget the peace of mind that I once sought.
You despise me, and I loathe you.
You are in a state of denial, but you know it's true.

I am overjoyed;
To avoid.
I'm proud that I've been shunned.
I am not stunned.

Standing in my corner is where I'll be.
You have always ignored me.
I'm going to make you pay attention.
Within every sentence you speak, my name you'll mention.

Extremely tart;
I am torn apart.
Expressed by way of art;
The most significant part.

I'm curious if you know.
If you are aware that you blow.
I've found strength to finally bathe.
You're able to be physically active; therefore, you I scathe.

Tremendously tart;
Right from the start.
I'll pull the trigger on three;
So you will depart.

Go purchase something for me to steal.
You are fake, but your humiliation is real.
On your pants is a circle of a secreted substance.
You are undeserving of sustenance.

Unequivocally tart;
When did it start?
Terrifically tart;
I have been ripped apart.

FOR VALENTINA

Valentina, you've given to me a great solution.
To you I am grateful for your prodigious contribution.
If you'll allow; then we will ignore what is common behavior.
Let us quickly indulge; You know it's you that I do savor.

I'm sure you know that perfection is derived from repetition.
We should repetitively practice not to return to the lonely condition.
It doesn't surprise me that you can't relate to my antisocial demeanor.
We shouldn't get along with anyone else because our minds are so much keener.

Valentina, you are more beautiful than any other.
I'm very clingy; please, do not mind if I tend to smother.
Since I have met you I've planned ahead and used facial cleanser.
You can even come with me when I visit my pharmaceutical dispenser.

She takes her time when she collects items of personal value.
Valentina steps back to select the things she must revalue.
Admire her for her cautious ways, and her femininity.
She hid her heart within the reassurance zone's vicinity.

Made in the USA
Columbia, SC
22 April 2020